Understan
Elephants

Guidelines for safe and
enjoyable elephant viewing

Elephant Specialist
Advisory Group (ESAG)

Published by Struik Nature
(an imprint of Penguin Random House
South Africa (Pty) Ltd)
Reg. No. 1953/000441/07

The Estuaries No. 4, Oxbow Crescent,
Century Avenue, Century City, 7441
PO Box 1144, Cape Town, 8000 South Africa

Visit www.penguinrandomhouse.co.za and
join the Struik Nature Club for updates,
news, events and special offers.

First published in 2017

10 9 8 7 6 5 4 3 2

Publisher: Pippa Parker
Managing editor: Helen de Villiers
Project manager: Colette Alves
Designer: Janice Evans
Proofreader: Glynne Newlands

Reproduction by Hirt & Carter
Cape (Pty) Ltd
Printed and bound by DJE Flexible Print
Solutions, Cape Town, South Africa

Print: 978 1 77584 341 2
ePUB: 978 1 77584 342 9
ePDF: 978 1 77584 343 6

Front cover: Elephant in full charge (Randy Hanna – visit
www.randyhannaphotography.com); Page 1: Sunset
(Francis Garrard); Page 8: Broken tusk (Lucy Bates); Page
34: Digging for water (Jeanetta Selier); Page 57: Throwing
debris (Jeanetta Selier); Back cover: (top) Testing for mating
readiness (Jeanetta Selier), (bottom left) Trunks entwined
(Lucy Bates), (bottom right) Herd walking (Lucy Bates)

Jeanetta Selier

Contributing authors

Marion E. Garaï	ESAG and Space for Elephants Foundation
Lucy Bates	University of Sussex, UK
Yolanda Pretorius	University of Pretoria, Centre for Wildlife Management
Michele Hofmeyr	South African National Parks (SANParks)
Michelle Henley	Save The Elephants – South Africa (STE-SA)/Elephants Alive (EA)
Jeanetta Selier	South African National Biodiversity Institute (SANBI)

CONTENTS

Preface 4

Introduction 5

Acknowledgements 68

Selected bibliography 68

PREFACE

This book examines elephant behaviour and provides guidelines on how to conduct yourself near elephants. It does not guarantee that you will never experience an incident in proximity to elephants, nor can it anticipate every situation or predict the behaviour of individual wild animals. Please take note of the Disclaimer on the imprint page.

Three maxims to keep in mind for a more enjoyable safari:
- Elephants are intelligent, have emotions and want mainly to be left in peace.
- Like all animals – including humans – elephants have a 'personal space', which they do not like invaded.
- You are in **their** home area.

In general, elephants will give warnings before launching an attack. These signs must be understood, respected and reacted upon.

As more and more tourists visit game reserves and are exposed to elephants, it is likely that the number of human-elephant encounters will increase correspondingly. On average, up to three people are killed annually in South Africa by elephants, and another three are seriously injured. The majority of these incidents could have been avoided had the people involved better understood elephant behaviour and been able to read the tell-tale signs. Remember, an attack is not just potentially tragic for the people involved: in many cases it leads to the demise of the animal too.

With this book we hope to provide readers with a better understanding of elephant behaviour and of how to avoid a negative or unfortunate encounter with these majestic animals. We offer suggestions on how to behave when driving near elephants, as well as how to react in difficult or dangerous situations.

At all times, elephants must be given right of way, and common sense and respect for the animals must prevail.

Yolanda Pretorius

INTRODUCTION

People have always been fascinated by elephants. Over the past 30 years elephants have been translocated to many private and state-owned reserves within South Africa, in order to make them more accessible to both local and international tourists. Initially, only young elephants were captured and translocated. However, once the technology of moving entire family units and large bulls had been mastered, the practice of moving juveniles alone was terminated and cow-calf groups, as well as larger bulls, were translocated following a specific set of regulations and preconditions. As a result, with the exception of the Kruger National Park Complex (including adjacent reserves that have dropped fences), Addo Elephant Park, Mapungubwe National Park and Tembe Elephant Park, elephants in all other reserves in South Africa have been brought in from elsewhere.

Translocation itself, as well as factors such as restricting fences, limited property size, human disturbance and encroachment on their habitat, have an adverse impact on the animals' mindset and social behaviour. These influences have been largely underestimated and poorly understood in the past. It is only now, after several decades of practising translocation, that consequential patterns of behaviour are being recognized.

Baby elephants are appealing but, for viewers' safety, must not be approached.

This book provides basic information on the normal behaviour, communication and interactions of elephants, and it also details the psychological and behavioural consequences brought about by social disruption. The enduring impact of early traumatic experiences, including Post-Traumatic Stress Disorder, is explained. Differences between a 'normal' population and a translocated one can be an important factor, particularly if you are driving in one of the smaller reserves in South Africa where elephants have been introduced relatively recently. Understanding these factors makes it easier to read abnormal or unpredictable behaviour.

Reported fatalities by free-roaming elephants (Aug 2008–Oct 2015)*	
COUNTRY	FATALITIES
Botswana	4
Cameroon	1
Ethiopia	1
Gabon	1
Ghana	2
Kenya	27
Liberia	1
Malawi	11
Mozambique	23
Namibia	5
South Africa	8
South Sudan	3
Tanzania	4
Uganda	3
Zambia	8
Zimbabwe	21
TOTAL	123
Approx. average per year	17.57

*News Service Save the Elephants
(www.savetheelephants.org)

Heike Zitzer

A bull reacting to the presence of a vehicle

Number of people killed or injured by wild or captive elephants in South Africa over a 20-year period (Approximate annual averages are also indicated.*)		
South Africa: 1994–2017	Total	Average per year
Fatalities from wild elephants	13	0.56
Injuries from wild elephants	17	0.74
South Africa: 1994–Jun 2015	Total	Average per year
Fatalities from captive elephants	6	0.3
Injuries from captive elephants	11	0.55

*Wentzel, I. & Hay, A. 2015. The National Council of SPCA's Welfare
of Elephants in Captivity in South Africa. Unpublished report. 32pp.

Number of people killed or injured by wild elephants in Mozambique over a 2-year period (Approximate annual averages are also indicated.*)		
Mozambique: Jul 2006–Sep 2008	Total	Average per year
Fatalities from wild elephants	31	15.5
Injuries from wild elephants	6	3

*Durham, K.M., Ghiurghi, A., Cumbi, R. & Urbano, F. 2010.
Human-wildlife conflict in Mozambique: a national perspective,
with emphasis on wildlife attacks on humans. *Oryx* 44(2) 1985-193.

Elephants spread their ears in response to the approach of a car.

PART ONE
Elephants
– the basics

CHAPTER ONE

ELEPHANT FACTS

Elephants are arguably Africa's most charismatic animals: their size alone makes them extraordinary, but their complex family life, their intelligence and their individual personalities set them apart too. This section deals with recognizing some of their more obvious characteristics, information that impacts on our viewing elephants and understanding their behaviour in the field.

Ageing and sexing elephants in the field

Knowing an elephant's sex and approximate age provides information about how it may behave: for instance, the oldest cow is the matriarch and will be the one to defend the group; young bulls can be boisterous and launch mock attacks; a female with breasts will likely have a small calf.

Age-related differences

- **Calves or infants under one year:** can walk under their mother's belly.
- **Calves up to two years:** are totally dependent on mother's milk. They are not capable of sucking up water with their trunk yet, and drink with their mouth.
- **Juveniles (2–10 years):** eat solid food although they will generally continue to suckle milk until the age of 3–4 years – or even longer if no new calf is born to the mother. During these years they slowly become more independent. **Males** play and spar with each other and will venture further away from their mothers. **Females** start to look after younger siblings – becoming 'allomothers'.

Calves under two years are not able to drink with their trunk, so use their mouth.

Babies younger than one year can walk under their mother's belly.

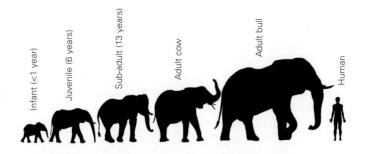

Infant (<1 year)   Juvenile (6 years)   Sub-adult (13 years)   Adult cow   Adult bull   Human

- **Sub adults (10–15 years):** in this phase **males** start to leave the family unit and associate more with other males; **females** engage in allomothering before their first conception. In translocated and socially disrupted groups, females can conceive as early as 5–7 years.
- **Adults (15-plus years):** these are now sexually mature elephants. **Females** generally give birth to their first calf; **males**, which are taller than females by this stage, but with a slender head compared to older males, have left the family unit to form associations with other males.
- **Adults 20–35 years:** the adult **female's** tusk circumference at the lip is now distinctly thicker than in younger females. From age 25 onwards, the **male's** head changes to an hourglass shape.
- **Adults 35–50 years:** the adult **female's** back has lengthened by now, is visibly longer, and her tusks are slowly thickening. Females over 50 years have hollows above their eyes; their ears are held low and they appear sway-backed. By age 40 years, the adult **male** is very big, with a heavy-set body, and towers over the largest female by 1 metre or more at the shoulder. His tusks are thick and the temple area has sunken in.

Lucy Bates

Juvenile females 'allomother', helping to look after siblings.

Lucy Bates

Juvenile males at play

Michelle Henley

Older males develop an hourglass-shaped head.

Lucy Bates

Older females develop hollows above their eyes.

Sexual differences

Both sexes continue to grow throughout their lives, but female growth slows down at about 25 years of age, whereas males continue to grow steadily. For a field estimate, an 18–20-year-old male is about the size of an adult cow, although there is considerable variation throughout the African continent as well as between individuals.

Mature male

Yolanda Pretorius

Mature female

Yolanda Pretorius

- much taller, with a *rounded* head
- tusks are thicker at the lip
- belly line slopes, and the penis sheath is visible
- 3.5–4m shoulder height
- weighs up to 6 tons

- smaller, with an *angular* forehead
- tusks are more slender
- belly line is more horizontal, and their breasts are usually visible
- 2.5–2.8m shoulder height
- weighs up to 3 tons

Seen from behind

The **male** has a ridge that extends from below the tail, down and in between the legs, and forms the penis sheath with its opening facing forward.

The **female's** vulva is squared off with the opening towards the ground, and the area under the tail is flat.

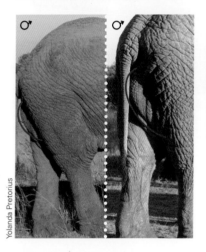
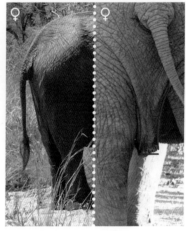

Seen from the front

The width of the trunk between the tusks is larger on males than on females.

Detecting elephants nearby

By being able to read the signs left by elephants you will be in a position to find the herd more quickly and know what to anticipate. You will be able to judge if they passed by long ago – and in which direction they went – or more recently, in which case they may still be nearby.

An elephant's front foot is rounder, while the back foot is more oval.

Elephants have the largest of all footprints, and their spoor is unmistakable.

Elephant spoor

Elephant footprints are unmistakable: they are the largest of all footprints, and leave a characteristically wrinkled or cracked, round or oval track. An elephant's footprints can give an indication of the animal's size: a rough approximation of shoulder height is equivalent to twice the circumference of the forefoot.

An elephant's front foot is rounder, its hind foot oval and slightly longer.

The hind foot usually imprints partly on top of the front footprint, and in front of it.

Direction of movement can be deduced by closer observation: the front edge, or toes, will make a deeper indent in the ground as the animal transfers weight onto this edge during lifting; and the back edge of the footprint is straighter than the more rounded front edge.

Speed can be inferred: the faster an elephant walks, the deeper the indent made by the front edge of its foot.

Consistent droplets of urine present in between the footprints of an elephant may indicate that it is a male in musth. These droplets normally have a very strong, musky scent. (See Chapter 3 for an explanation of musth.)

Elephant dung

Elephant dung boluses are usually deposited in a loose pile if the animal is resting or foraging; if deposited while on the move, the dung boluses will be spread out in a line along the path of movement.

Generally, a female elephant's dung bolus is smaller than that of a male, and the female's urine marks are closer to, or almost on top of, the dung.

Elephant dung can most easily be confused with rhino dung, but it can be distinguished by its lighter and/or more reddish colour when fresh, as well as being more fibrous – containing more and longer 'unchewed' fibrous material.

Black rhino dung generally has distinctive woody stem fragments of the same size, cut off at an angle of 45°, whereas white rhino dung consists purely of finer grass fragments. Both rhino species use communal dung-heaps, and they often scrape the dung with their feet for dispersion. Their boluses are more triangular than those of elephants.

Elephant dung is redder than rhino dung.

Rhino dung is darker and triangular.

Elephant dung is more fibrous.

Rhinos defecate in a communal spot.

Foraging signs

Elephants remove bark from tree trunks at between 1 and 2 metres in height, or they strip bark from smaller stems. Although the sap dries quickly, the branch will be pink in colour (for most tree species) if it has been recently stripped.

Forcefully broken-off (not cut off with teeth), discarded tree branches and uprooted plants or grass tufts that still have fresh, unwilted leaves are a sign that foraging elephants have recently passed by.

Discarded mopane branches are evidence of elephants having foraged.

Elephants strip bark from tree trunks, leaving exposed, wound-like areas.

Uprooted and broken trees are evidence of elephants having passed through this dry landscape in search of food.

Lucy Bates

Features such as a broken tusk make it possible to identify individual elephants.

Identifying individual elephants

When regularly visiting a specific area occupied by elephants with a view to studying them more closely, find out as much as possible about the history of that particular population of elephants. To a large extent, this knowledge should dictate how you behave around the group, and what cues to look out for to avoid a potentially aggressive interaction.

Furthermore, within that population, it is useful to be able to identify individual animals and learn about those individuals' personal histories. For example, some bull elephants have been translocated, sometimes more than once, and/or have been deterred from lodges by various methods. Such interventions could either make them more aggressive towards humans or have habituated them to the extent that they have lost their natural fear of us.

By taking careful note of their characteristics, you will be able to recognize individual animals simply from their facial features, as you would an old friend!

Ears

Elephants live in harsh environments, so they do, on occasion, tear their ears, sometimes catching them on thorn trees; tears can also occur when bulls fight one another. The resulting scars and tears – frayed edges, rips, or holes – are distinctive and can be used to identify individual elephants.

The vein patterns in the ears differ from one individual to the next, and can also be used for identification.

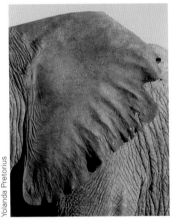

Each elephant has differences in vein patterning on the ears.

Tears and scars on ears help us identify individual animals.

Tusks

The size, shape and direction of growth of the tusks can all be used to identify an elephant.

Some elephants do not have tusks, or they have broken one or both of them, making for unique and easily identifiable characteristics.

An elephant with a skew tusk

A female with a broken tusk and torn ear

Other marks

Often elephants have distinctive bumps on their trunk or body, derived from old injuries. For example, part of the tail or trunk may be missing, or their legs may have wounds from snares, making them easily recognizable.

A trunk with a snare attached

A snare wound on the leg

This individual has a very distinctive large lump on the side of its body.

Wrinkles

Some elephants have distinctive wrinkle patterns on their forehead.

An elephant's wrinkles, close up

Distinctive forehead patterns

An elephant herd makes its way through water to reach the bank Ian Whyte

Elephant social grouping

African elephants live in complex societies characterized by different levels of social and spatial relationships among individuals and groups. The social environment of an elephant encompasses the entire subpopulation of an area; this generally consists of several clans, comprised of family groups that share a common home range during the dry season.

Understanding the many behaviours shown by elephants is deeply rewarding. Some of the questions raised may be: are they playing or seriously fighting?; who is the mother of a calf and who are the additional carers?; what is happening between the sexes?; who is the matriarch and what is she doing? The following chapters address such questions.

Depending on the type of social unit you come across you will have to be more or less wary: cow herds with tiny calves will be more nervous and therefore more defensive; lone old bulls, especially during their 'musth' period, must be avoided; large herds will be less nervous than small herds.

CHAPTER TWO

FAMILY GROUPS AND FEMALE BEHAVIOUR

African elephants live in a matriarchal, or female-dominant, society. Their well-organized and close-knit family units are subsets of larger, looser aggregations, or clans, sharing a common home range.

Family groups, or cow-calf units (also known as breeding herds), form the basis of elephant society, consisting of an older matriarch, her dependent offspring, her adult daughters and their offspring – the group varying in size from two to more than 20 individuals.

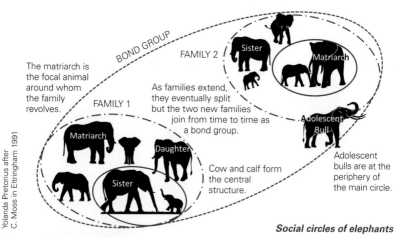

BOND GROUP

FAMILY 2

Sister

Matriarch

The matriarch is the focal animal around whom the family revolves.

As families extend, they eventually split but the two new families join from time to time as a bond group.

FAMILY 1

Matriarch

Daughter

Adolescent Bull

Cow and calf form the central structure.

Sister

Adolescent bulls are at the periphery of the main circle.

Yolanda Pretorius after C. Moss in Eltringham 1991

Social circles of elephants

Jeanetta Seiler

Greeting with trunks

When a family group increases in number beyond the capacity of its environment, it splits up to form two groups, with the most closely related individuals staying together. Within a population, certain family groups have stronger bonds with each other and these so-called 'bond groups' are thought to be relatively close blood relations.

When related or known family groups meet up they engage in elaborate greeting ceremonies: they approach enthusiastically, entwining trunks,

Jeanetta Seiler

Females in a family group attend to a baby.

rumbling, trumpeting and bellowing, twirling around in circles, bumping parts of their bodies together, streaming from their temporal glands, urinating and defecating, smelling and stroking each other with intense interest.

A female typically spends her entire life in her natal family group, the individuals of which are therefore generally very closely related and form strong bonds with each other. Members of a family group spend most of their time together, engaging in similar behaviours, such as feeding, drinking or mud-bathing, with brief periods of separation for foraging.

Lucy Bates

A family group rests in the shade, with the baby protected in the middle.

The role of the matriarch

The matriarch is usually the oldest (and largest) cow in the unit and has a great responsibility towards the group. She is the hub around which everything revolves. She leads, defends and keeps the unit together, and is responsible for major decisions such as where to go and when to move. Often, she will stand guard when the family crosses roads.

As the oldest female in the group, the matriarch has the greatest environmental knowledge, such as where to find water in the dry season, and where and when to find the most nutritious food. She knows which other species can be dangerous, such as lions; and she can also distinguish between human voices and, according to her experiences with humans (e.g. poaching, being hunted or captured) and the perpetrators of such experiences, may react differently to male or female voices.

Just as important is her social knowledge, such as recognizing which other elephant families are friendly and which are to be avoided. A matriarch can recognize up to 100 other females in the population just by their voices. The rest of the family relies heavily on her knowledge.

The matriarch passes on all this knowledge to her offspring. If a matriarch dies before her time, the unit loses valuable environmental and social knowledge and may even disintegrate.

Families with a young matriarch are less likely to survive droughts and are generally more at risk. If the matriarch lives to a ripe old age, then her eldest daughter (or a sister) will most likely take over the position, having had time to accumulate sufficient experience and knowledge.

In a translocated group the matriarch has to start from scratch to accumulate knowledge, and this places an excessive amount of stress on her.

Choosing partners for reproduction

In order to ensure the best genes for her offspring, a female chooses which male may mate with her. The older the female and the higher her rank, the more selective she can be when it comes to mating.

Mounting

Jeanetta Selier

Females prefer to mate with older, bigger males, and males with larger tusks, as they have proven to be strong and to have good genes. Younger females often have to be content with younger males, but can be prevented from mating by the matriarch, who may chase these young bulls away.

Lucy Bates

A protective female with her offspring

Elephant pregnancy

Gestation lasts about 22 months and a cow may suckle an existing calf right up until she gives birth to her next offspring. The calving interval is typically four years, depending on the individual's age, health, the habitat and climate. The interval is known to have been as long as nine years in extreme drought conditions and as short as two-and-a-half years in translocated elephants.

Culls, habitat reduction and, above all, translocations have altered these socialization patterns, thereby causing severe social disruption, along with behavioural consequences.

Calves and juveniles

During their early years, calves and juveniles are the centre of the unit. Calves of both sexes are embedded within the family unit and taken care of by many other females. These are generally older female siblings or

Jeanetta Selier

Family members greet and inspect a new calf.

Juveniles play, strengthening bonds and establishing dominance hierarchies.

Females will often stand in a circle to protect resting babies.

cousins; they will eagerly help their mother, older sister or aunt look after any new calf, play with it and take care of it while the mother feeds or is otherwise occupied. These caretakers are called 'allomothers'.

Elephant calves are never alone – young female elephants love to be near the babies, so there are always several allomothers in attendance. Allomothers often wake the calves from their regular naps so as to ensure that they are ready to leave with the herd, and to keep up with them. Calves remain dependent on their mother and the care of allomothers for many years.

Suckling

Calves suckle on average for 3–5 years, but start tasting solid food at about 3–4 months. They lack sufficient co-ordination of their trunk, as well as strength, to be able to survive on solid food without milk until they are about two years old.

Jeanetta Selier

Suckling not only provides milk, but is also a source of comfort for the young. A mother will allow a calf to suckle after it has experienced a stressful situation. Comfort suckling is also known to be given by allomothers, both young and old, even though they have no milk.

Suckling provides milk as well as comfort.

Touching

A mother and calf will frequently touch each other with the trunk and trunk tip. Allomothers and other family members also 'inspect and touch' the babies frequently.

Mother touches calf	Calf touches mother or other family member
Mothers and allomothers frequently touch the calf at the mouth, ears, genitals and anus.	A calf expresses its affection for its mother, but also obtains information, e.g. what its mother or sister are eating. A calf will touch its mother when it wants to suckle.
The mother obtains chemical information on the well-being of the calf (e.g. its stress level, its state of digestion, what it has eaten etc.).	A calf will also obtain chemical information and in this way learn about nutritional and social aspects, such as what to eat and how to assess the state of other elephants.
Most importantly, touching has a great calming effect on the calf.	

A female reassures and calms a young calf with the touch of her trunk.

Jeanetta Selier

A mother protectively stops her baby from approaching a vehicle.

Jeanetta Selier

The importance of allomothering

Allomothering benefits both calf and the allomother. A calf is highly vulnerable and needs the protection and guidance of the other family members. It has been shown that the more allomothers a calf has, the higher its chance of survival.

Young females love to be near babies and spend much time engaging in allomothering, which is as important for them as it is for the babies. It teaches them how to raise a baby. First-time mothers that have not had allomothering experience because of social disruption such as translocations have been shown to be less successful at raising their young, and have even been known to kill their calf.

Allomothers care for a newborn.

Jeanetta Selier

A long juvenile period

Calves are protected throughout their long juvenile stages by all the females in the family. When there is perceived danger, or when the calves are resting, the adults create a defensive circle around them.

Young elephants, like human children, take a long time to grow up and have much to learn: how to interact socially with other elephants, how to fit into the dominance hierarchy, whom to respect, and how to

A mother assesses a vehicle while calves sniff for clues.

Jeanetta Selier

Lucy Bates

Adults form a defensive circle around calves.

Nervous elephants arrange themselves to encircle and protect the babies.

communicate. They must also learn a variety of possible future roles: females learn how to become allomothers, mothers or matriarchs; males learn how to behave towards other males, how to deal with musth, etc.

Sexual differences in early behaviour

In early life, play is very important for both sexes.

Female calves have a different focus from early on. Because they remain within their natal group all their lives, they are continuously exposed to the matriarch's knowledge and well placed to learn about their future roles.

Young males tend to be more adventurous and boisterous than their female siblings and spend more time at a greater distance from their mother. They start joining and sparring with other young males, thus preparing for the dominance hierarchy within a future bull society, and for the greater independence they will later have to cope with.

Males grow up in a female-dominated society until puberty (12–15 years). After puberty, they associate more with other and older bulls, and may be chased out of the unit by the older females. This transition usually takes place over several months as the young bull tries to find his place within the male society, while still spending time with his natal group.

CHAPTER THREE

MALE BEHAVIOUR

As they grow up, males pass from one kind of society to another, very different one. A juvenile graduating to adult male society has to learn how to conduct himself in the new order: how to fit into the male hierarchy, how to deal with 'musth', how to behave towards older bulls and how to gain access to females for reproduction.

Male elephant society

Once a bull has left his natal family unit he will join up with other bulls in a bachelor group. Bulls have a different, but equally complex social organisation. Old bulls can accommodate being solitary more easily, while younger bulls are dependent on the company and mentorship of older bulls.

The dominance rank among bulls in a given area is ascertained through sparring, and the hierarchy is strictly adhered to. The size and strength of the bulls is, therefore, the controlling factor. The occurrence of musth (described on p.30) also plays a significant role in the dominance hierarchy.

Bulls associate with cow-calf groups randomly and will move between groups in search of oestrus females – those that are sexually receptive. Once a bull has found a suitable female, he will 'test' her urine and genitals, using his trunk tip to carry the cow's scent to a specialized gland (Jacobson's organ) in the roof of his mouth. In this way he assesses information on her hormonal state (i.e. whether she is ready for mating).

Bulls sparring

Michelle Henley

If he is interested, he shows it by standing behind her and placing his trunk over her back. The courtship, involving occasional matings, lasts up to a few days, with the bull guarding the cow against the solicitations of other contenders. The penis is very long and S-shaped in order to reach the ovaries, which are situated relatively far inside the female.

Age increases a bull's reproductive success. In natural conditions, bulls usually start having regular annual musth cycles at around 25, and reach their prime at about 40 years of age. It is at this age that they become the preferred mates of oestrus females.

A male testing a female

A bull courts a cow, showing his interest by putting his trunk on her back.

The bull's penis needs to be long to reach the cow's ovaries.

Translocation fallout

Translocated bulls are usually moved singly or in pairs, which results in the total loss of their social unit. As young bulls in normal elephant society reach musth age (around 25 years), they begin to spar with and dominate younger bulls, and to mate with oestrous females. But, if there are no other suitably aged bulls available – or perhaps no other elephants at all – frustration can cause young bulls to seek alternative outlets. These can be in the form of an attempted break-out from captivity, pushing down trees, or aggression towards substitute opponents such as vehicles, people or even rhinos.

How to recognize 'musth'

Being in a state of musth denotes a period of great physiological and behavioural change in the life of a bull. During this time, testosterone hormone levels in the blood of a male increase (up to 50-fold compared to non-musth levels) and, as a result, the bull becomes more aggressive.

André Ganswindt

A musth bull with temporal gland secretion and a whitish-green penis sheath

> *During this period both other bulls and humans are wise to keep their distance.*

During musth the temporal gland (situated between the eye and the ear) frequently secretes a dark, oily fluid, which runs down the cheek of the elephant to the corner of the mouth. In full musth, the temporal gland is swollen to the size of an orange and is clearly visible. Some bulls' glands may even swell to the size of a soccer ball! The penis is sheathed and a constant dribbling of urine can be seen. When displaying dominance during musth, a bull may specifically unsheath his penis and gush urine. The penis and the area around the sheath may look whitish-green because of all the discharge; the insides of the legs become darkened with fluid. Bulls urinate onto their legs so as to spread the smell. This urine leaves a scent spoor on the ground, which is picked up by other elephants. Even humans can detect the distinct smell of both musth secretions from the temporal gland and urine.

Michelle Henley

The penis sheath of a bull in musth

A musth bull with a visibly swollen temporal gland

A musth bull with urine constantly dribbling on his back legs

The following visual signs are frequently observed in musth males, although they can occur – to a lesser extent – in non-musth males too:

▨ **Ear wave:** moving one ear at a time. The inner and upper portion of the ear is thrust forward vigorously, followed by the outer lower part, creating a wave across the ear. The sound from these sharp earflaps is similar to the cracking of a whip.

▨ **Marking:** rubbing the temporal gland area against trees.

▨ **Musth walk:** the head is carried high, well above the shoulders, with the chin tucked in. The ears are often tensely spread and carried high. There's a controlled swinging motion of the head and tusks.

▨ **Tusking:** males go down on their knees and tusk the ground or vegetation, or throw bushes and other objects at vehicles or other elephants.

▨ **Musth rumble:** a very low rumble performed with an ear wave. A loud earflap sounds like the crack of a whip and marks the end of the vocalisation.

▨ **Draping the trunk:** males drape their trunk over one of the tusks, especially while they're walking; this is thought to release some of the pressure on the temporal glands.

Musth bull walking with head held up

Onset of early musth

When there are no older bulls present and the social hierarchy has been disrupted though translocation, young bulls will come into musth at a much earlier age, possibly in their teens. This has been a big problem on some reserves, where the young musth bulls tend to show aberrant behaviour and kill rhinos and other large game. In most cases the introduction of older bulls will alleviate this problem.

Andrew Blackmore

Heike Zitzer

Ear wave

A bull and cow flirting with each other

Yolanda Pretorius

Temporal gland secretion

Lucy Bates

Adult male with folded ear and temporal gland secretion

Frequently asked questions about musth	
Questions	Answers
Is a musth bull dominant over other bulls?	Yes, he is highly aggressive during this time and dominant over all other non-musth bulls.
How long is a bull in musth?	A musth period can last from a few days to a few months, depending on several factors (e.g. the animal's age, number of other bulls in the area, climatic conditions, body condition and the bull's position in the hierarchy).
What is the purpose of musth?	Musth helps the male secure a more dominant position within the bull hierarchy and gives him better mating opportunities, as an experienced cow will give preference to a bull in musth over other bulls. During this time the bull actively seeks out receptive females and mates with them.
When do bulls first come into musth?	The first onset of musth occurs normally when a bull is in his mid-twenties and from then on recurs once a year. Males under the age of 25 years are unlikely to come into musth, provided there are older bulls in the population.
Are bulls that are not in musth capable of mating?	Yes, non-musth bulls are also capable of mating.
Why do bulls show their musth so distinctly?	This signals that other bulls ought to stay away from a bull in musth, and avoid confrontation, and at the same time allows interested oestrous females to know his state.
Is an elephant that secretes from the temporal gland always in musth?	Both males and females can sometimes be seen to secrete from the temporal gland (between the eye and the ear) and this alone does not indicate musth. This normal temporal gland secretion (TGS) is of a different chemical composition to the musth secretion and is more watery. It also lacks the distinct musth smell.

PART TWO
Understanding elephant ecology and behaviour

CHAPTER FOUR
ECOLOGY AND THE ENVIRONMENT

The size of these megaherbivores has a double edge: the animals themselves must cope with the stresses of their gigantism, and the environment must accommodate their over-sized requirements and considerable impact.

Coping with cooling

Elephants have to be careful of overheating in hot weather.

The larger the volume of a body, the smaller its relative surface area, so that even though elephants have massive bulk, they have a *relatively small surface area*. Their body will heat up only slowly but, once warm, it cannot lose heat rapidly.

Elephants lack sweat glands, so they can't get cool, as humans do, through perspiration and evaporation. However, they have developed other mechanisms for keeping cool:

- An increased surface area promotes heat dissipation; elephants achieve this with their large ears and wrinkled skin.
- Flapping their large ears creates a breeze, which cools the blood in the many small veins and vessels in the outer ear – creating a built-in fan. In hot weather, elephants will increase their ear flapping, even when resting, thus constantly cooling off.
- Although elephants have very few sweat glands, they can lose water through their skin by diffusion. A young elephant can thus lose up to 2.5 litres of water every hour, an adult probably twice as much. This diffusion not only helps the elephant keep cool; it is also important to keep the horny outer layer of the skin moist and supple.
- Elephants will bathe at any opportunity. The body stays cooler eight times longer after being plastered with mud than when it has just been sprayed with water. Elephants therefore need water and the opportunity to mud-wallow.
- Apart from water and mud, elephants will use any item in the habitat such as sand or even grass to throw and blow onto themselves with their trunk, showering it all over the body, back, legs, belly and face. This helps keep the skin moist and prevents sunburn.

Mud splashing

Mud bathing

Swimming

Sand bathing

Rubbing

Improving habits

After a good mud-wallow, elephants will frequently rub their bodies against objects such as tree stumps or rocks. This cleanses the skin of parasites, which become embedded in the mud and then scraped off. Any available object will do for scratching!

Habitat requirements

Knowing something about the habitat and ecology requirements of elephants will enable better understanding of what they are doing and where to find them. It also helps understand any large-scale impact on plants that you might come across – visible signs of elephants having been present, such as disarranged branches, uprooted trees, scratchings, etc.

Water

Elephants require fresh water daily. A trunkful of water amounts to around 5–10 litres and an elephant will drink 100–200 litres per day.

In dry conditions, elephants, with their extraordinary ability to smell underground water, will dig in dry riverbeds and uncover underground pools. They visit these waterholes daily, and they are also used by other mammals, which are not able to dig such deep holes. Typically, elephants excavate the sand with their front feet and trunk, then carefully suck up the water with their trunk. The water that seeps into the hole is filtered through sand particles, so it is often particularly clean and much favoured.

Digging for water

Various family groups may meet and drink together at a river.

Feeding on thorn trees is no problem; they readily eat thorns, leaves and stems.

Nutrition

An adult bull will consume 300–400kg of fresh forage per day, a cow about 250kg. This means that an elephant consumes about 6–8% of its own body weight daily. It digests only about 30–45% of what it eats, since fermentation takes place in the hind gut, which is a less efficient system than that of rumination employed, for example, by cattle. This explains why elephant dung boluses contain a high percentage of undigested plant matter.

Although elephants' preferred diet is fresh grass, they will also browse on leaves. Twigs, bark and roots form part of the diet too, especially in the dry season when no grass is available. It is highly likely that browse is critical to enable maximum energy potential for fermentation.

Because elephants can tolerate a relatively poor quality diet, they are found across many habitats, from verdant to arid. In harsh regions and adverse climatic conditions, however, they need more time and larger quantities of food to obtain the required nutrients and energy. Large bulls are more tolerant of poor-quality diets, but need more bulk relative to females.

In times of food stress, elephants will debark trees and ingest the bark, which provides nutrients such as minerals and fatty acids. They also push over trees to get to the nutritious roots and top leaves. Despite having a very sensitive mouth, elephants can tolerate thorns on *Acacias*.

Digging for salts

In mineral-poor areas, elephants often supplement their mineral deficiencies by eating soil and digging for salt. Of course, like all animals, including humans, elephants have certain favourite plant species, and will target these 'ice-cream' species first. This can be a problem on a reserve where rare habitats or plants may be over-utilized.

Juveniles learn what to eat by checking what their mother is feeding on.

The effects of elephants on vegetation

Elephants, along with other animals such as the rhinos, hippos and giraffes, are known as megaherbivores – those weighing more than 1,000kg. Elephants are so-called 'keystone' species, which means they are able to change the habitat they live in and function as drivers in various ecological processes that can influence other species. These changes need not be negative: nature is never static and changes in the vegetation open up new opportunities.

Droppings

The large quantities of dung deposited by elephants play a major role in the recycling of nutrients. On average, an elephant will deposit around 100kg of dung per day. This amounts to 37 tonnes of manure per km² (assuming that there is one elephant per km²).

Dung contains large proportions of undigested seeds, and these can provide nutrition for other animals such as baboons. The fibres in the dung also provide food for termites, which in turn provide food for other species.

Dung beetles are wholly reliant on dung. They carry it to their nests for food, and roll perfect balls of it in which to lay their eggs. When their larvae emerge, they find a ready-made pantry from which to feed.

Elephant dung fibres

Dung beetles carry elephant dung to their nests.

Seed dispersal

Seeds and fruits consumed by elephants are dispersed away from the mother plants. Seeds of certain plants such as *Acacias* germinate much better if they have passed through the gut of an animal such as an elephant, as the enzymes in the gut soften the seeds' hard outer coat.

Tree pushing and debarking

Elephants are often accused of being 'destructive'. This is a value judgement: elephants impact on their habitat in relation to the natural resources available. If the natural resources are manipulated by humans (e.g. by the provision of artificial waterholes), elephants' impact may be more pronounced and lead to changes in habitat composition and structure, especially in localized areas close to artificial waterholes. Looking at the bigger picture, though, elephants may be increasing the diversity of the ecosystem by creating patches of heavily utilized vegetation where elephant-tolerant species can thrive, interspersed with so-called refuge areas far away from water where more elephant-intolerant plant species grow.

Elephants remove bark from branches with their tusks to obtain nutrients.

Although elephants do push over trees to reach the browse, roots and bark, tree pushing can also be a dominance display, especially by males – much like gorillas slapping their chest. Elephants that are stressed and pressured by tourist vehicles have been known to push trees onto roads to prevent vehicles from following them. They have also been seen to push trees down onto electric fences to short-circuit the electricity, so they can step over the fence.

We often notice when large trees have been removed, although this has been happening for eons, but fail to see the more subtle disruptions in complex cyclical ecological patterns. For example, frequent fires started by humans prevent young trees from growing, and artificial water points attract high densities of smaller herbivores, which feed on tree seedlings.

Ecosystems are constantly changing, and change is necessary for habitats to evolve.

Positive effect of pushed-over trees

Studies reveal that the utilization patterns of elephants give us indicators as to what nutrients are available where and when. This helps in management processes.

A tree that has been pushed over is a biome in itself; a dead tree can be home to a myriad frogs, geckos and insects, which may feed from the early-morning mist traps spun by spiders.

Trees are not always dead when pushed over, but can coppice (resprout), with the new shoots or buds often having a higher nutrient content than before. The smaller herbivores are then able to browse off vegetation not usually available to them. Black rhinoceros and other browsers are able to reach foliage they may desperately need during the dry season, and the downing of trees opens up grassland for many herbivores.

Dead trees provide nutrients to the soil and can prevent erosion in bare areas. Pushed-over trees provide cover for saplings of shade-dependent trees and grass species to grow, and protection from small browsers.

On the other hand, habitats from which elephants have disappeared can also change significantly: open grassland will revert to woodland and thicket, and this has a marked effect on the distribution of other species.

True habitat destruction happens only when there is a serious over-population and the animals have nowhere to move to, for example, within small fenced reserves.

Breaking the trunk of a tree can make new growth available to smaller browsers.

41

Home ranges and migration patterns

Elephants are not territorial. However, each family or clan has a specific home range, and these may overlap. Elephants can walk vast distances in search of nutritional forage and water, and to find salt licks with their special minerals, so that home ranges will vary according to the time of year, habitat and climate. They can be as small as 15–50km^2, or as large as 500–3,000km^2 – sometimes even larger. However, with the erection of fences, these long-established elephant migratory patterns have become greatly restricted.

Elephants walking and foraging in their home range

Jeanetta Selier

Plants that elephants find most palatable

Elephants are broad-spectrum megaherbivores and will feed on a wide variety of trees and shrubs, switching from grass grazing in the wet season to browse and bark-stripping during the drier months. However, they do prefer some plants to others.

Plants preferred by elephants

Grewia

All *Grewia* (raisin) bushes

An upright, straggly shrub, growing to 3m in height. It is a vigorous, many-stemmed climbing shrub or can even grow into a small tree reaching 5m in height. Sought after by breeding herds.

Acacia

Acacia trees (knobthorn and fever tree)

Deciduous trees reaching 20m in height. Usually leafless during winter and early spring. Elephants feeding on these trees strip off large sections of bark, which often results in the trees being ringbarked and eventually dying.

Ana tree

Ana tree *Faidherbia albida*

Large, deciduous, cold-resistant tree; fast-growing to 30m. It likes waterlogged soils along rivers, swamps, floodplains and dry river courses. Attracts insect-eating birds. The pods are high in starch and excellent fodder for game and stock; the seeds have high protein content. This is a protected tree in South Africa.

Sycamore fig

Fig trees (e.g. sycamore fig *Ficus sycomorus*)

A large, spreading, semi-deciduous to evergreen tree, growing to 25m tall and 30m wide. Widespread along Lowveld rivers. The figs are eaten by bats, birds, antelope, warthogs, monkeys and elephants. All parts of the tree are widely used medicinally or as a food throughout Africa. As with the *Acacias*, decimation of these beautiful trees in the ecosystem is serious.

Baobab *Adansonia digitata*

This massive iconic tree grows to 25m in height. A slow grower, it prefers drier, low-rainfall areas. Targeted by elephants because of the high moisture content in the bark and central pith of the trunk. This tree is less affected by elephants as it cannot be ring-barked, although it is generally destroyed by them when repeated feeding breaks down the trunk structure and the tree collapses.

Baobab

Marula tree *Sclerocarya birrea*

A distinctive bushveld tree growing to 15m in height; deciduous and fairly fast growing. The fruits are high in vitamin C and are sought after by elephants and other species such as baboons and monkeys during the summer months. The leaves are also taken by a large variety of animals. Elephants feeding on the bark of these trees may ring-bark them, which leads to the eventual death of the tree.

Marula

False thorn tree *Albizia* species

Medium to large deciduous trees, some growing up to 18m in height, with a spreading canopy, resembling *Acacia* trees but without thorns. Leaves are browsed by elephants and antelope. The trees have soft wood and are often completely consumed by feeding elephants. The main trunk is also susceptible to ring-barking by feeding elephants.

False thorn tree

Despite persistent reports of elephants getting drunk on rotting marula fruits, there is little scientific evidence to back this up. Elephants rarely, if ever, eat marula fruits that have fallen to the ground and begun to rot – they prefer fruit fresh from the tree. Also, many other animals eat these fruits, so it is unlikely that they would be left to rot. Even if an elephant were to eat a few, they would have little impact on their digestion. Indeed, scientists have calculated that an elephant would have to eat over 1,400 well-fermented fruits in one sitting to begin getting tipsy.

Mopane tree *Colophospermum mopane*

A medium to large deciduous, slow-growing, woody tree up to 18m in height. Food plant of the mopani worm, larva of the emperor moth (*Gonimbrasia belina*). The leaves and pods ranks high in the elephant diet, also eaten by cattle and game. In areas of high elephant browsing, they can form coppice thickets, often dominating the landscape.

> *Cussonia* and *Erythrina* species are also much enjoyed by elephants, as are many aloe species.

Mopane

What elephants find unpalatable

There are very few species that elephants will **not** eat if they are suffering food stress in a long dry season, but if alternatives are available the following species will be less targeted.

Euphorbia species

All of these species contain a thick milky latex that is toxic and unpalatable. The latex can cause intense skin and eye irritation and can even cause blindness. Tree-like succulents, growing to 10m, usually on rocky outcrops.

Guarrie tree *Euclea* species

These have thick, leathery evergreen leaves and may not be very tasty. A shrub or small tree that grows to 1–4m in height; multi-stemmed and densely branched. Occurs in dry bushveld and riverine thickets and on hot rocky ridges.

Euphorbia

Kudu lily *Pachypodium saundersii*

A succulent shrub that resembles the impala lily, but differs by having sharp, slender spines along its branches and stem, which is enlarged, silvery and gnarled. Grows to 1m, occuring in dry woodland and rocky areas. The spines may be a deterrent to elephants but the sap is also very bitter.

Guarrie

Spike thorn tree
Gymnosporia heterophylla
These also have thick and leathery evergreen leaves and may not be very tasty. Usually a shrub but occasionally a small erect tree up to 4m in height. Occurring at low altitudes in open woodland and stony places. It is common in open bush in the lowveld and arid lowveld.

Ted Woods

Spike thorn

Impala lily *Adenium obesum*
A succulent, fairly cold-resistant, deciduous plant that can grow to 4m high in favourable conditions. Thick, carrot-shaped underground tuber. Sap is bitter and toxic, and has been used on arrows and for poisoning fish.

Ted Woods

Impala lily

> Beechwood (*Faurea saligna*) is also a common species not touched by elephants.

Elephants and humans
In South Africa, in particular, elephants are confined within fences, and some reserves have a high tourism density. These factors impact negatively on the elephants' behaviour and movements, as well as on the vegetation. This, in turn, requires intensive management.

The effects of humans on elephants
Human activities such as tourism, hunting or other intrusive behaviour can change elephant distribution and utilization patterns, as well as affecting their behaviour, making these animals more wary and nervous.

Elephants react to tourist pressure by avoidance behaviour, increased mobility, bundling together and showing increased levels of stress hormones. Consistently high levels of such hormones may negatively affect their physiology and breeding ability.

Management interventions such as contraception (either through immunocontraception, vasectomy or hormonal treatment) may influence both the physiology and behaviour of elephants.

Fencing reserves

Before fences were erected, elephants could migrate over vast distances, thus allowing vegetation along the way to recover before the herd revisited the area. These routes often went over mountains. Most of our modern-day road passes are built on old elephant migration paths, as they selected the easiest and best routes across such barriers.

Today, fences, roads, towns and other man-made constructions have severely fragmented the once vast habitat of elephants in South Africa. Confinement to a fenced-in, relatively small reserve has serious consequences for the social behaviour of elephants, as well as for the local vegetation. Fences prevent gene flow among many species, and stop elephants from interacting with their greater social circle, which promotes unhealthy inbreeding. Specific habitat areas are adversely affected when the elephants are prevented from moving away to find alternative feeding grounds. Within small reserves there are often multiple artificial waterholes that further change the seasonal movements of elephants and increase the impact on rare local tree species.

Anso le Roux

Elephants at a fence

Jeanetta Selier

A tourist vehicle parked too close to elephants

CHAPTER FIVE

COMMUNICATION

Elephants have diverse ways of communicating, about which there is still much to discover. Understanding some of their methods helps us to 'read' elephants and anticipate what reactions to expect from others in the herd.

Jeanetta Selier

Elephants often use their back feet to explore objects and each other.

Tactile communication

Elephants are extremely tactile, as is apparent in family bonding and between adults and calves. They touch each other not only with their trunk, but also with their ears, tail, head and whole body. This is clearly communicative: they are aware of their bodies and don't bump or touch one another unknowingly.

Touching with trunks is especially eloquent: elephants entwine trunks as a form of greeting and to solicit play. An elephant placing its trunk tip into the mouth of another is showing subordination. This behaviour also serves to calm any conflict when bulls play-fight, indicating that the fight is not serious.

Even merely standing close to each other is also a way of showing who likes whom.

Adults discipline youngsters with their trunk, shoving, slapping or pulling them. A mother will frequently touch her calf with her trunk, foot or tail. A calf solicits suckling by touching its mother's back, belly, legs or nipples.

Trunks entwine for play or in greeting.

A mother reassures her calf.

A trunk in another's mouth is submissive.

Chemical communication

Elephants have an excellent sense of smell and rely heavily on chemical cues, such as pheromones, which convey both short- and long-distance information. From a combination of chemical signals, elephants obtain information about each other's presence, emotional and physical states and, to some extent, the trails over which they have passed.

Testing genitals for hormone information

They are able to recognize individuals by smell, and frequently touch each other's genitals, mouth, ears, temporal glands, dung and urine with their trunk tip, thus obtaining information concerning each other's health, reproduction status and emotional state.

Elephants will often lift their trunk tip and rotate it in all directions, 'testing' the air. Depending on the wind direction, they can detect the

presence of other elephants, or of danger, over great distances. If the gesture is directed at tourists, it might be a signal of unease (see Chapter 7).

Elephants also gain chemical information by sniffing other elephants' urine on the ground. The urine trails of oestrous females or musth bulls leave distinct signals, serving to attract interested partners, or to keep competitors away in the case of musth. To this end, musth males will also rub temporal gland secretions against vegetation.

Trunk lifted to test the air

Visual communication

Elephants' sight is less well developed than their senses of hearing and smelling, but is not as bad as commonly thought: elephants do use visual displays and signals to inform or influence one another over short distances.

Their body language incorporates:
- **Threat displays:** behaviour such as spreading their ears and lifting their head to appear larger for an opponent.
- **State announcement:** body stances, such as holding the head high or the 'musth walk', communicate to others what state an elephant is in.
- **Communication of intent:** this can also be visual, such as purposefully moving in a specific direction to motivate others to follow.

A juvenile plays at display behaviour

A bull sniffs to assess a nearby vehicle.

A group of elephants with spread ears, a clear threat display

Jeanetta Selier

▓ **Show of frustration:** often when a subordinate elephant is shoved away by a more dominant one, he or she will display frustration by a shake of the head or throwing a stick.

Audio communication

Vocal communication is a highly sophisticated and complex way of sending and obtaining information over both short and long distances.

Elephants have a large and varied repertoire of vocal sounds, ranging from trumpeting to infrasonic calls too low for human hearing. Approximately 30 distinct calls and their meanings have been deciphered. Different calls are used to coordinate group movements and/or to warn others of danger (e.g. poaching or culling) and they function as contact calls when group members are dispersed over large areas.

Female elephants can distinguish calls of family or bond group members from those of 'outsiders'. Matriarchs are able to distinguish about 100 different individuals by their call alone. Playback experiments have shown that elephants can distinguish individual voices from a distance of up to 2.5km; and that they react to calls up to 4km away, while on clear, calm, relatively cold nights their hearing range can probably reach as far as 10km.

An elephant that is listening will raise its head, spread its ears and 'freeze'.

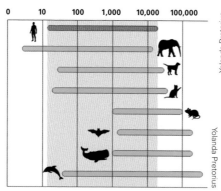

	0	10	100	1,000	10,000	100,000
Human 20–20,000Hz						
Elephant 5–12,000Hz						
Dog 50–45,000Hz						
Cat 45–65,000Hz						
Mouse 1,000–100,000Hz						
Bat 2,000–120,000Hz						
Beluga Whale 1,000–120,000Hz						
Dolphin 75–150,000Hz						

Hearing range comparison (adapted from philtulga.com)   *Listening*

Yolanda Pretorius

Some easily recognizable and audible elephant calls include:

- **Rumbling:** a low sound, much like that of a far-off engine. Rumbles include an infrasonic component, possibly as low as 5–8Hz (human hearing extends only to about 30Hz), which can be heard over a distance of 4km or more.
- **Trumpeting:** a high-pitched sound produced by forcing air through the trunk. This can act either as an alarm to other elephants or as a warning to chase off intruders. Elephants are also known to trumpet extensively when they meet up with other elephants, when they approach a waterhole or when they are playing.
- **Growling/roaring:** a loud, guttural sound produced with the mouth open and the head lifted, and often directed towards a disturbance. This sound is produced when an elephant is annoyed or frustrated. A calf may roar out of anger when prevented from suckling.
- **Screaming:** very young elephant calves can be heard to scream when in panic. Adults may do the same, but this is rarely heard.

For further information on audio communication go to http://www.elephantvoices.org

Seismic communication

Seismic waves travel through the ground and are picked up through special sensory corpuscles in the feet and trunk tip of elephants, possibly up to a distance of 32km. Such waves caused by thunderstorms can be picked up by elephants from as far away as 160km. They are also able to pick up waves caused by other individuals that may be running or charging, or even very low-frequency rumbles. Elephants engage in 'freezing behaviour' when detecting seismic information, and may sometimes lift a front foot off the ground to facilitate localization of sound.

Yolanda Pretorius

Front foot swinging could indicate either an assessment of vibrations from the ground or indecision.

Interspecies communication

Recent experiments with captive elephants show that they understand human pointing and can use such information as an indicator of where they should search for food. The only other animals known to follow human pointing, such as dogs and horses, have been domesticated for millennia.

CHAPTER SIX

NEUROLOGY, INTELLIGENCE AND THE EFFECTS OF TRAUMA

Elephants have the largest brain of all terrestrial animals, a fact that has probably contributed to their reputation for long memories and superior intelligence. In relation to their body size, elephant brains are comparable in size to those of great apes, but are smaller than human and dolphin brains.

An elephant brain contains as many cortical neurons (specialized cells in the cortex of the brain) as a human brain, but elephant neurons are larger than those of humans and have the potential for many more connections. These extra connections between brain cells could support greater learning and memory skills.

What elephants know about their physical world

Lucy Bates

A large herd migrating to find better resources

Mental maps

Elephants appear to have exceptional mental mapping skills, and are reliant on the long-term memories of older individuals who can recall the locations of distant food or water sources last visited many years earlier.

Savanna elephants often have to cover very large distances to find sufficient food and water. Elephants in both the Namib Desert and in Mali are known to travel several hundreds of kilometres to reach remote waterholes shortly after the onset of rain, by way of routes that they may not have followed for several decades.

Research shows that families with older matriarchs are better able to survive periods of drought, and are better able to avoid predators. A lifetime's learning is key for elephants.

Tool use and insight

Elephants are capable of making and using tools for a range of functions, such as scratching themselves, removing ticks and swatting away flies.

Recent experiments with captive elephants suggest they can also solve problems by insight, rather than by actively trying out a range of different solutions before finding the right one (trial and error).

What elephants know about their social world

What they know about other elephants

Social knowledge accrues with age; the older the individuals, the greater their social understanding. Elephants form alliances and coalitions with other members of their group, and can work together to solve problems. For example, individuals may work together to rescue an elephant that is trapped in a drainage ditch, to retrieve a calf that has been 'kidnapped' by another elephant family, or to support elephants that have been darted for veterinary purposes.

Elephants recognize other elephants as distinct individuals, and keep track of where each family member is.

Analysis of wild elephant behaviour shows that they understand the emotions and intended goals of others: elephants have empathy. They help and comfort others who are distressed or in danger, and attempt to help troubled or dying elephants.

What elephants know about themselves

Most animals (except humans and great apes) simply view their image in a mirror as that of another animal, and react to it in a social manner. However, one elephant housed in a zoo in New York passed the mirror self-recognition test: it removed a dab of paint from its own head that it could not have known was there without seeing it in the mirror. This

Caressing an elephant skull

elephant recognized the mirror image as being itself. So perhaps elephants, like humans and great apes, but unlike any other mammal, have a concept of self.

Elephants have some sense of death. They mourn their family members and will come back to caress, touch and sometimes cover, the remains of known elephants. They do not do this with the bones of other animals.

The brain and emotion

All mammals share the same basic physiological and emotional traits, such as fear, aggression and anxiety. From rodents to humans, we all have a limbic system – a generalized 'emotional brain' responsible for coordinating stress-response behaviour and integrating sensory information, which has changed little through the evolutionary stages.

The neuron pathways in mammals' brains retain 'memories' of experiences. Repeated or intense negative experiences, such as a capture operation or the culling of a group of elephants, results in the memory becoming 'engraved' in their brain, requiring only a small trigger to reactivate the memory and generate consequent behaviour.

How trauma and stress manifest

There is a critical relationship between social development and brain development.

Capturing babies

If a young animal experiences the break-up of social bonding or suffers trauma and deprivation (such as separation of mother and calf, or being subjected to a capture and translocation operation), then abilities to self-regulate and engage in typical friendly behaviour are diminished. These developmental patterns can persist through adulthood. Symptoms will likely surface when stress or deprivation levels increase beyond a certain point, such as observed in the 'flashbacks' characteristic of Post-Traumatic Stress Disorder (PTSD).

A young elephant kicks up dust as it charges in warning.

Jeanetta Selier

Flashbacks

Individuals with PTSD experience flashbacks. These are memories of a past traumatic event that are relived periodically, activated by unconscious triggers. A small input such as a smell, sound, sight or movement can trigger the flashback, and the animal relives the trauma, which it perceives as real.

This can explain the sometimes irrational or erratic aggression displayed by elephants that have previously experienced a serious trauma or stress in their lives, such as being translocated or in some other way persecuted (for example, through poaching).

PART THREE

How to watch
elephants safely

CHAPTER SEVEN
SIGNALS TO LOOK OUT FOR

Elephants are very communicative. Through different types of vocalisations, chemical signals, body postures and movements, or touching each other with their trunks, they 'talk' to each other, communicating how they feel, what they want to do, warning about impending danger, reprimanding their calves, etc. The better you can read these signals and take precautionary measures, the safer you will be – and the more enjoyable the elephant sighting.

Relaxed and friendly behaviour

Elephants with no aggressive intentions will go about their daily business and ignore any human observer. In general, their eyes will be cast down. A calmly feeding elephant will look at the ground or the tree it is feeding on. The tail will generally sway from side to side while the elephant is feeding. Other signs of relaxed behaviour are entwining trunks or placing the trunk tip into another elephant's mouth – both are reassuring gestures used for greeting and in play behaviour.

Elephants can discreetly observe vehicles or their occupants while feeding, by twisting their trunk tip in the direction of the disturbance, or slightly raising their ears to listen, and even looking in that direction without turning their head.

Friendly interaction with heads held low

Lucy Bates

Michelle Henley

Family resting, flapping ears to cool down

Adult male sniffing while feeding

Trunk in mouth

Signs of uneasiness or apprehension

▦ **Trunk up in the air:** 'sniffing the air' is the most obvious sign that the elephant is aware of your presence.

▦ **Plucking at vegetation but not really feeding, slapping the vegetation against a part of the body:** elephants do naturally shake off earth or dirt from plucked vegetation, but in an exaggerated form, this displacement behaviour is indicative of uneasiness or conflict. The elephant is pretending to be feeding, but at the same time will be watching the situation – called 'displacement feeding'.

▦ **Throwing twigs or stones:** this is the next step in a conflict; the behaviour could escalate into something more aggressive.

Female sniffing and assessing a potential threat

Shaking soil off grass

Front foot lift

Biting own trunk

A tail twisted and held up to the side indicates that the elephant is nervous.

- **Foot swinging:** one forefoot is raised and tentatively swung backwards and forwards. This suggests being unsure of what to do next: should I confront or retreat?
- **Touching own face:** the trunk is swung upwards and touches or rubs the animal's own face. This is used as self-reassurance in a conflict situation or when feeling uneasy.
- **Tail raising:** the tail is raised and slowly starts curving towards the side in a stiff, unnatural manner.
- **Trunk twisting:** the trunk tip is twisted back and forth and shows uneasiness.
- **Biting the trunk:** holding the trunk in the mouth suggests being unsure of what to do next.

CHAPTER EIGHT
WARNING SIGNALS AND SIGNS OF AGGRESSION

Each individual animal has a 'personal space' which can differ in size depending on the animal's emotional state, experience and the particular situation.

The very outer comfort zone

This is the area or distance that an animal requires in order to feel comfortable about the presence of other animals. When you are outside the animal's personal space, you do not pose a threat. The animal is unperturbed and carries on with its normal activities.

→ No apparent threat to either party.

Anso le Roux

Elephants in relaxed, friendly state

The alert zone (outer zone of personal space)

You have entered the animal's personal space; it is aware of you. The animal may 'freeze' to conceal itself and analyse the situation. Responses vary from approaching, out of curiosity; continuing to show no interest by resuming the original activity; or moving away.

→ Confrontation is usually avoided in this situation.

Lucy Bates

Juvenile displaying

The warning zone

You have penetrated the second personal zone and the animal may begin to feel uncomfortable or threatened. An elephant may respond by displaying warning signs – this is to persuade the intruder not to come any closer. With ears spread and head up, it may vocalize, shake its head, flap its ears against its body, raise its tail, break branches, throw sand or branches, kick dust, and even make a mock charge.

Threat display: tail up, ears spread

→ If you back off, the animal will usually calm down and possibly move away.

Threat display, pointing tusks towards the perceived threat

The critical or attack zone

If you ignore the warning signals, the intensity of the elephant's response will increase; following this, the animal may run away if there is an available escape route, or more likely it will attack in defence.

→ Serious injuries can occur as a result of failure to take adequate precautions.

Head shaking shows annoyance.

Elephants run in response to a helicopter above.

Signs of threat display and aggression

An elephant will warn you if you are too close and it wants you to retreat. It is essential to be able to 'read' the first warning signs; if these are not heeded, the elephant may resort to more aggressive threat behaviour, or may even launch a charge – mock or otherwise – without other warnings.

Threat display

At any of the the following signs, you must retreat slowly. If, once you have retreated, the signs persist or other signs are displayed, leave the area immediately and give the elephant space.

▨ **Ear spreading:** facing an opponent, spreading the ears out (at 90 degrees to the body).

▨ **Standing tall:** lifting the head high, well above the shoulders, to appear taller. The chin is raised and the elephant looks down at its adversary.

Ear slapping

▨ **Head shaking:** an abrupt nodding, jerking or tossing of the head that causes the ears to flap. Generally light at first, this can become more vigorous, and shows great annoyance.

▨ **Trunk swung forward:** swinging or tossing of the trunk towards an opponent or a small animal. (This can also be play behaviour in very young elephants.) Musth males use an exaggerated trunk swing towards another male while blowing air, creating a loud 'whooshing' sound. But if the trunk is swished towards your vehicle, it generally means 'go away – you are in my personal space'.

Shaking head, throwing grass, challenging the viewer

▨ **Trumpeting or air blast:** trumpeting is often a show of annoyance, although calves use it in play. The trunk can also be used to blow air out with a loud popping sound.

▨ **Ear slapping against their body:** an ear is slapped against the side of the body, creating a popping sound. This is a threat signal towards people or cars.

▨ **Throwing dust, branches or objects:** lifting an object and throwing it in the direction of an opponent; elephants' aim is accurate.

Swinging trunk forward

A serious charge by an adult female

Tree pushing

Tusking the ground

Rushing forwards in a mock charge

Bush bashing: tossing of the head and tusks through the bush or vegetation, creating quite a commotion and demonstrating strength. Young elephants use this in play too.

Tree pushing: although this is generally done in order to get to tasty parts of the tree, it can also be a show of strength or redirected aggression, especially by males. In this case, they do not feed on the tree, just push it over.

Tusking the ground: bending or kneeling down and tusking the ground, pushing their trunk along the ground or uprooting vegetation – another form of redirected aggression. It can also be seen as a demonstration of what the elephant intends to do to you if you do not respect its space. Males are more likey to use this behaviour. Cows may also go down in a kneeling position, but on their back legs.

Pointing tusks: tusks pointed towards you, ears spread, the animal prepares to move towards you at speed – this is a serious threat.

Rushing forwards: a mock (warning) charge involves rushing towards an opponent or vehicle, ears spread, then stopping abruptly, kicking up dust with a forefoot, swinging the trunk towards the opponent or vehicle. Often trumpeting or an air blast is heard.

Real charge: rushing towards the opponent or vehicle, ears spread, trunk usually tightly curled under, head held low, tusks directed towards the opponent. A real charge is very fast and comes suddenly, without warning; it can be silent or accompanied by trumpeting.

CHAPTER NINE

HOW TO CONDUCT YOURSELF AROUND ELEPHANTS

Elephants always have right of way!
Respect their personal space!

In areas where they have been exposed to regular game drives, elephants are usually habituated towards people. However, in areas where they have been harassed, hunted, culled, poached or recently translocated, they need to be given more space.

How to watch elephants from a vehicle in safety

Do's

✔ Slow down as soon as you see elephants; do not rush up to them. When approaching or leaving a sighting, never drive faster than an elephant can walk (5–8km/h).

✔ Place your car in such a manner that, if possible, people in other vehicles can also see the elephants.

Beware of elephants

Yolanda Pretorius

✔ Make sure your vehicle is not boxed in; keep an escape route open, preferably forwards – it is difficult to reverse out of an aggressive situation.

✔ If other vehicles misbehave, rather leave the scene and plan to come back later. Report bad behaviour of other observers to management.

✔ If the elephants show any signs of apprehension or unease, retreat from the sighting slowly and steadily.

✔ If the temporal glands of cows have started streaming, you are too close for their comfort and you should give them more space, irrespective of the existing distance between them and yourself.

✔ Back off calmly if you see any threat behaviour, to give the elephants more space and let them continue with their natural activities; when the situation has settled again, switch off the engine, sit quietly and enjoy.

✔ However, if they continue to show apprehension or their threat behaviour intensifies, drive away SLOWLY and quietly.

✔ Speak in hushed tones and avoid making jerky movements.

✔ Watch both sides of the bush and keep an eye on your rear-view mirror. An elephant could sneak up from behind and block your escape route.

✔ Back off slowly if an elephant approaches closer than within 20m of your vehicle.

✔ Allow a bull in musth extra space and watch his behaviour particularly carefully. If in doubt, rather move off slowly.

✔ Reverse to move away from a musth bull that is in front of you; do not drive past him.

✔ Be aware that musth bulls have a habit of advancing straight towards the vehicle when they spot you. In particular, if they are with a breeding herd, they will pointedly come towards you to assert their dominance. The rest of the herd will carry on with life as usual if you have approached them in a respectful manner and if you are quiet while watching them.

✔ Always keep in mind that bad behaviour from people who have visited the herd before you, or previous trauma experienced by the herd or individuals within it, might affect the way the elephants will react to being watched.

✔ When you have seen enough, move away from the sighting SLOWLY!

Babies with trunks entwined

Don'ts

✘ Never speed past a herd of elephants.

✘ Never drive closer than within 50m of the nearest elephant.

✘ Never box elephants in; if there are other vehicles at the sighting, always ensure the animals have an escape route.

✘ Never drive in between members of a herd that has spread out on either side of the road: if mothers become separated from their calves, they can become aggressive.

✗ Never switch the engine off in order to let the car roll towards the herd, as this may startle them; it is better to let them know you are there, let them hear, smell and see you, so that they can choose to remain or move away with ease.

✗ Never try to divert elephants as they are walking, and do not try to usher them out of the way by driving too close behind them.

✗ Never rev the car engine as the noise upsets them. Some people use this tactic to 'push' elephants off the road or to assert their own dominance; habitual exposure to this type of behaviour may make elephants aggressive towards innocent onlookers too.

✗ Never drive off the road to get a closer look.

✗ Never bang the side of your vehicle or make other noises to attract the attention of the elephants or to get a good photograph.

✗ Never persistently follow any herd and especially not a musth bull!

✗ Never allow an elephant to come too close to your vehicle; should this happen inadvertently, keep still, don't make a noise and allow the animal to pass by.

✗ Never encourage close encounters; even though they might be unforgettable and special experiences, such encounters may endanger the lives not only of tourists, but also of elephants as they may react badly and subsequently have to be put down.

✗ Never approach elephant bulls: every time a vehicle has a close encounter with a bull, the particular animal gains confidence to the point where he may test his strength against a vehicle in the future.

✗ Never assume that because the elephants were well behaved on previous sightings, they will behave in the same manner this time.

How to react in the event of a close encounter

✳ If an elephant approaches your vehicle closely and you are stuck and unable to leave the area, stay calm, breathe deeply, do not make jerky movements or suddenly try to start the vehicle or honk the horn. Speaking to the elephant slowly in hushed tones can indicate that you are calm and not a threat.

✳ If you are ever in a situation where you are being charged and cannot immediately leave the area, you can break the elephant's concentration momentarily by tapping (not banging) on the vehicle door and raising your voice slightly. Try to maintain calm and slow tones – not aggressive or high-pitched, which could make the situation worse. Most elephants will stop to reassess the situation once their concentration has been broken by an unexpected response from the observer. This may afford you an opportunity to leave.

ACKNOWLEDGEMENTS

The following people readily supplied photographs and are to be sincerely thanked for the free use of these: Lucy Bates, Andrew Blackmore, Stephan Cilliers, Jasper Cloete, Shem Compion, André Ganswindt, Marion Garaï, Francis Garrard, Randy Hanna, Michelle Henley, Lucy King, Anso le Roux, Brett Mitchell, Yolanda Pretorius, Ingo Schmidinger, Jeanetta Selier, Space for Elephants Foundation, Heike Zitzer and Ian Whyte. A special thanks goes to Ted Woods for the tree photos. Some pictures of postures and threat signs were acquired with kind permission from Joyce Poole and Petter Granli of Elephant Voices.

Yolanda Pretorius supplied the drawing of social circles and the diagram of elephant ages and is to be sincerely thanked.

SELECTED BIBLIOGRAPHY

Bradshaw, G.A. 2009. *Elephants on the Edge*. Sheridan Books, USA.

Elephant Voices. http://www.elephantvoices.org

Eltringham, S.K. (Consultant). 1991. *Elephants: Illustrated Encyclopaedia* Salamander Books Ltd. Ldn, NY.

Hoare, R. 2001. A Decision Support System for Managing Human-Elephant Conflict Situations in Africa. African Elephant Specialist Group (AfESG), Species Survival Commission (SSC), IUCN.

Kangwana, K. (Ed). 1996. *Studying Elephants*. AWF Technical Handbook Series 7. African Wildlife Foundation, Nairobi.

Moss, C. 1988. *Elephant Memories*. Elm Tree Books.

Moss, C.J., Croze, H. & Lee, P.C. (Eds). 2011. *The Amboseli Elephants. A Long-term Perspective on a Long-lived Mammal*. University of Chicago Press, Chicago.

O'Connel, C. 2007. *The Elephant's Secret Sense*. Oneworld, Oxford, UK.

Payne, K. 1998. *Silent Thunder*. Jonathan Ball, Johannesburg.

Poole, J. 1996. *Coming of Age with Elephants*. Hodder and Stoughton, UK.

Preller, B. 2015. *The Silent Giants of Southern Africa*. www.silentgiants.co.za

Shoshani, J. 1992. *Elephants: Majestic Creatures of the Wild*. Weldon Owen Pty Ltd., Australia.